Wilson Reading System®

Student Workbook
Three A

THIRD EDITION

by Barbara A. Wilson

Wilson Language Training Corporation
www.wilsonlanguage.com

Wilson Reading System® Student Workbook Three A

Item # SW3A

ISBN 978-1-56778-084-0

THIRD EDITION (revised 2004)

The Wilson Reading System is published by:

Wilson Language Training Corporation
47 Old Webster Road
Oxford, MA 01540
United States of America

(800) 899-8454

www.wilsonlanguage.com

Printed in the U.S.A.

April 2006

Read the first syllable with the second syllable. Cover the divided word and write the word on the line. Uncover the divided word and check spelling. Read the written words.

bas - ket   = _____

in - dex   = _____

cob - web   = _____

cab - in   = _____

hab - it   = _____

mag - net   = _____

fin - ish   = _____

sun - set   = _____

pan - ic   = _____

nap - kin   = _____

Read the first syllable with the second syllable. Cover the divided word and write the word on the line. Uncover the divided word and check spelling. Read the written words.

whip - lash   =   _____

un - zip   =   _____

pic - nic   =   _____

pub - lic   =   _____

up - set   =   _____

ad - mit   =   _____

pun - ish   =   _____

rob - in   =   _____

rel - ish   =   _____

nut - shell   =   _____

Read the sentence. Select the correct word from the box to complete the sentence. Write the word on the line. Reread the completed sentence. Use each word in the box only once.

picnic	finish	bathtub	relish	happen
rubbish	chipmunk	magnet	napkin	cactus

1 Bill and the kids will go on a _____.

2 Fran had fun with the _____.

3 We must get this pup in the _____.

4 I think the _____ has a nut.

5 Kevin had a _____ plant for his mom.

6 Mom must get _____ for the hot dogs.

7 Did Stan _____ to win the trip?

8 We must _____ this job and then rest.

9 Get the _____ and dump it in the trash can.

10 At lunch, Tom had a _____ on his lap.

Read the syllables on each side of the box. Draw a line to connect syllables to form real words.

tom	lin		top	ic
gob	lic		nut	cot
pub	cat		mas	meg

ox	sil		ex	ic
pun	en		pan	it
ton	ish		pig	pen

Write the words above on the lines below. Read the words.

_____   _____

_____   _____

_____   _____

_____   _____

_____   _____

Read the syllables on each side of the box. Draw a line to connect syllables to form real words.

mus	ten
mit	tang
al	bum

hel	gun
shot	fin
muf	met

rab	nic
nap	bit
pic	kin

bas	it
fin	ket
hab	ish

Write the words above on the lines below. Read the words.

Divide each word below into syllables. Read the word. Write the syllables on the lines.

upset = _____ _____

topic = _____ _____

habit = _____ _____

relish = _____ _____

hatbox = _____ _____

mustang = _____ _____

muffin = _____ _____

undid = _____ _____

zigzag = _____ _____

velvet = _____ _____

puppet = _____ _____

Underline or "scoop" the two syllables. Mark the syllables with a **c** to indicate a closed syllable. Put a breve (˘) above the vowels. Read the words.

EXAMPLE: <u>sŭn</u> <u>fĭsh</u>
    c   c

nutshell	muffin	cobweb
tennis	submit	catfish
picnic	mix-up	cannot
edit	unless	combat
satin	public	shellfish
nutmeg	Edwin	polish
cotton	Boston	Dallas
denim	punish	tonsil
sudden	pollen	seven
pocket	hiccup	Texas

Read the sentences. Find the multisyllabic words by "scooping" or underlining syllables.

1   the dog in the bathtub is a mess

2   did Justin get upset when he fell in the slush

3   fred has a pack of gum in his pocket

Write the sentences correctly on the lines below. Add capital letters and punctuation. Proofread carefully.

1 _____

_____

_____

2 _____

_____

_____

3 _____

_____

_____

Read the first syllable with the second syllable. Cover the divided word and write the word on the line. Uncover the divided word and check spelling. Read the written words.

in - sult = _____

in - dent = _____

snap - shot = _____

hun - dred = _____

fish - pond = _____

den - tist = _____

in - tend = _____

drop - cloth = _____

plas - tic = _____

sand - box = _____

trans - mit = _____

milk - man = _____

Read the syllables on each side of the box. Draw a line to connect syllables to form real words.

chip	dred
hun	tist
den	munk

sand	lot
rad	dren
chil	ish

in	sist
crick	vent
in	et

ex	drop
gum	press
span	dex

Write the words above on the lines below. Read the words.

_____   _____

_____   _____

_____   _____

_____   _____

_____   _____

Read the sentence. Select the correct word from the box to complete the sentence. Write the word on the line. Reread the completed sentence. Use each word in the box only once.

splendid	blindfold	contest	handstand	clinic
gumdrop	sandwich	insist	plastic	talent

1 I will get a ham _____ for lunch.

2 I think Mom will _____ that I do this math.

3 Bob has lots of singing _____.

4 Get the _____ cup for a drink of tonic.

5 Ben must win the next _____.

6 Janet did the best _____ on the grass.

7 This dress is _____!

8 Sid had the last _____ in the dish.

9 Janet went to the _____ to get a check-up.

10 I have a _____ and I can not see.

Select a syllable from the top of each box to form real words. Write the syllables on the lines. Read the words.

mat	span	den

_____ dex

_____ tress

_____ tist

chil	ab	pil

_____ grim

_____ dren

_____ sent

top	in	chip

_____ munk

_____ sist

_____ most

tic	kin	et

plan _____

fran _____

pump _____

lem	et	tic

plas _____

crick _____

prob _____

bag	on	ic

hand _____

clin _____

drag _____

Divide each word below into syllables. Read the word. Write the syllables on the lines.

shipment = _____ _____

insult = _____ _____

spinach = _____ _____

disgust = _____ _____

insist = _____ _____

expand = _____ _____

clinic = _____ _____

triplet = _____ _____

intend = _____ _____

plastic = _____ _____

trumpet = _____ _____

disrupt = _____ _____

Divide each word below into syllables. Read the word. Write the syllables on the lines.

handstand   =   _____   _____

wellbred   =   _____   _____

express   =   _____   _____

gumdrop   =   _____   _____

fishpond   =   _____   _____

wingspan   =   _____   _____

bobsled   =   _____   _____

slingshot   =   _____   _____

sandblast   =   _____   _____

handbag   =   _____   _____

snapshot   =   _____   _____

wildcat   =   _____   _____

Find the two-syllable words. Underline or "scoop" the two syllables. Mark the syllables with a **c** to indicate a closed syllable. Put a breve above the vowels. Read the words.

EXAMPLE: <u>cŏn</u> <u>tĕst</u>
    c   c

1 Ted will win the next contest.

2 I intend to shop for a goblin mask.

3 The handstand contest was fun.

4 Find the pumpkin in the sandlot.

5 The children must rest on the bunk beds.

6 Don will attempt to hit the bell with the slingshot.

7 Dad was frantic when he lost his cash.

8 Did Fred get that grandslam hit?

9 A windmill is at the top of the hill.

10 That bat had a six-inch wingspan.

Nonsense Words

Underline or "scoop" the two syllables. Mark the syllables with a **c** to indicate a closed syllable. Put a breve (˘) above the short vowels. Read the nonsense words.

EXAMPLE: <u>wĭg</u> <u>glĕt</u>
    c   c

wigglet	flonnich	triddop
shupnest	shiblent	chinfrob
drennist	frentlap	troppit
plabbid	thibselt	fleppen
trendid	plimmut	trilmest
flidden	drappog	enflont
clupnet	thipnest	instom
podjift	timplet	contimp
stroplim	greffib	extrib
glisset	vambith	admest

Read the sentence. Select the correct word from the box to complete the sentence. Write the word on the line. Reread the completed sentence. Use each word in the box only once.

ostrich	nonstop	contest	fishpond
insist	pretzels	upset	wingspan

1 Ted will win the next _____.

2 The _____ can run fast in the sand.

3 That bat had a six-inch _____.

4 Ken was _____ when he lost the cricket in the grass.

5 Dad will get the _____ jet to Dallas.

6 We had chips, tonic, _____ and dip.

7 Did Dad _____ that Ben take a nap?

8 Bring your fishing rod to the _____.

Read the first syllable with the second syllable. Cover the divided word and write the word on the line. Uncover the divided word and check spelling. Read the written words.

con - tact = _____

ex - pect = _____

ob - ject = _____

sus - pect = _____

dis - tract = _____

in - spect = _____

con - duct = _____

sub - ject = _____

ex - act = _____

in - sect = _____

Read the sentences. Underline or "scoop" the two-syllable words to divide them.

1   I expect to win the next contest.

2   This subject is lots of fun.

3   We must inspect the trash for the lost mitten.

4   The insect is in this bucket.

5   Can you distract Jill?

Write the words containing the **ct** blend on the lines below. Write the whole word on the first line. Then divide the word into syllables on the second line.

ct

1 _____   _____ _____

2 _____   _____ _____

3 _____   _____ _____

4 _____   _____ _____

5 _____   _____ _____

Read the sentence. Select the correct word from the box to complete the sentence. Write the word on the line. Reread the completed sentence. Use each word in the box only once.

expect	insects	conduct	subject	distract

1 Ned had bad _____ in math class.

2 I _____ to be back at six o'clock.

3 There are lots of _____ in the trash can.

4 Spelling is my best _____.

5 We will _____ the kids in Mr. Smith's class.

Copy each sentence above on the lines below. Proofread carefully.

1 _____

_____

2 _____

_____

3 _____

_____

4 _____

_____

5 _____

Read the sentence. Find the two-syllable words. Underline or "scoop" the syllables in the two-syllable words.

1 that insect bit kim on the leg

2 i suspect that we will get lots of sun

3 beth has that exact pin

4 can we inspect the desks with mr. chang

5 mr. flint will contact jeff

Write the sentences correctly on the lines below. Add capital letters and punctuation. Proofread carefully.

1 _____

2 _____

3 _____

4 _____

5 _____

Nonsense Words

Cross out any nonsense syllable if it is **not** closed. Find and underline all closed syllables and mark them with a **c** to indicate closed. Mark the short vowels with a breve(˘). Read the closed syllables.

EXAMPLE: <u>clŭp</u>
     c

bract	prine	chait
toip	flet	nect
ust	flict	blish
neg	min	fle
shene	trat	shemp
prog	fect	trung
com	stoad	crobe
fleam	pless	pect
ish	ject	und
vect	ble	clend

Combine the syllables to form a real word. Cover the divided word and write the word on the line. Uncover the divided word and check spelling. Read the written words.

Wis - con - sin = _____

At - lan - tic = _____

es - tab - lish = _____

mis - con - duct = _____

fan - tas - tic = _____

ath - let - ic = _____

pen - man - ship = _____

hob - gob - lin = _____

Thanks - giv - ing = _____

bas - ket - ball = _____

Divide each word below into syllables. Read the word. Write the syllables on the lines.

Wisconsin = _____ _____ _____

Atlantic = _____ _____ _____

establish = _____ _____ _____

misconduct = _____ _____ _____

fantastic = _____ _____ _____

athletic = _____ _____ _____

penmanship = _____ _____ _____

hobgoblin = _____ _____ _____

Thanksgiving = _____ _____ _____

basketball = _____ _____ _____

Select a syllable from the top of each box and write it on the line to form a word.

gob	tab	hab

es _____ lish

hob _____ lin

in _____ it

sis	ket	tas

as _____ tant

bas _____ ball

fan _____ tic

pen	ish	con

pun _____ ment

ap _____ dix

Wis _____ sin

com	lan	con

At _____ tic

ac _____ plish

dis _____ nect

Write the words above on the lines below. Read the words.

_____

_____

_____

_____

_____

_____

_____

_____

Read the sentence. Select the correct word from the box to complete the sentence. Write the word on the line. Reread the completed sentence. Use each word in the box only once.

| disconnect | penmanship | fantastic | athletic | punishment |

1 I have the best _____ in this class.

2 Jim and Peg had a _____ picnic lunch.

3 Ken got a _____ for misconduct.

4 Can you help me _____ this?

5 Ed has the best _____ skill.

Copy each sentence above on the lines below. Proofread carefully.

1 _____

2 _____

3 _____

4 _____

5 _____

Underline or "scoop" the syllables. Mark the syllables with a **c** to indicate a closed syllable. Read the words.

athletic	sandwich	contest
hundred	planet	Wisconsin
fantastic	plastic	Atlantic
trumpet	appendix	disconnect
hobgoblin	establish	inhabit

Write the words with three syllables on the lines below. Read the words.

_____   _____

_____   _____

_____   _____

_____

Read the sentence. Find the three-syllable words. Underline or "scoop" the three syllables and mark them with a **c** to indicate closed.

1   glen went to the athletic contest

2   mr. griffin must get his appendix out

3   ed had lots of stuffing on thanksgiving

4   the basketball contest was fantastic

5   can sid disconnect the old TV

Copy each sentence above on the lines below. Add capital letters and punctuation. Proofread carefully.

1 _____

_____

2 _____

_____

3 _____

_____

4 _____

_____

5 _____

Add the suffix to each baseword. Write the whole word on the line. Read the word and circle the suffix.

crash - ing   =   _____

spell - ing   =   _____

stack - ing   =   _____

click - ing   =   _____

limp - ing   =   _____

thank - ing   =   _____

spill - ing   =   _____

sniff - ing   =   _____

crush - ing   =   _____

camp - ing   =   _____

Add the suffix to each baseword. Write the whole word on the line. Read the word and circle the suffix.

rust - ed = _____

dent - ed = _____

squint - ed = _____

mind - ed = _____

blend - ed = _____

fold - ed = _____

test - ed = _____

blind - ed = _____

plant - ed = _____

trust - ed = _____

talent - ed   =   _____

invent - ed   =   _____

disrupt - ed   =   _____

insist - ed   =   _____

inspect - ed   =   _____

punish - ing   =   _____

contract - ing   =   _____

distract - ing   =   _____

finish - ing   =   _____

expect - ing   =   _____

Read the word. Cover it and write the baseword and the suffix on the lines. Check your spelling.

crashing = _____ - _____

blinded = _____ - _____

punishing = _____ - _____

rusted = _____ - _____

distracted = _____ - _____

spelling = _____ - _____

squinted = _____ - _____

contacted = _____ - _____

planted = _____ - _____

inventing = _____ - _____

insisting = _____ - _____

expected = _____ - _____

1 Ken is standing with his hands in his pockets.

2 Get the fishing rods in the shed.

3 The kids are singing six songs.

4 We will be dusting the cobwebs.

5 Jill invented this fantastic plan.

Write the words containing a suffix on the lines below.

1 _____ _____ _____

2 _____ _____

3 _____ _____ _____

4 _____ _____

5 _____

Underline or "scoop" the syllables and circle any suffixes (**ed**, **ing** or **s**).

smelling	slingshot	rested
clocks	splashing	basketball
plastic	distracted	spinach
tennis	dumping	drums
invented	planets	disrupting

Write the words with a suffix on the lines below. Read the words.

_____   _____

_____   _____

_____   _____

_____   _____

Vocabulary Practice

Write sentences with each vocabulary word below. Use a dictionary or electronic spell checker as needed. Underline each syllable in the vocabulary words.

3.1	3.2	3.3	3.4
index	talent	contact	athletic
topic	contest	inspect	penmanship
panic	intend	expect	establish
submit	disrupt	subject	misconduct
admit	expand	distract	inhabit
exit	invent		
publish	frantic		
solid	insist		
oxen	insult		
habit	splendid		

Story Starter

At the end of Step 3 create a story that includes many (at least 5) of the vocabulary words below. This story takes place in a park. Underline each vocabulary word used from the list below.

upset	talent	suntan	fantastic
zigzag	sandlot	hundred	wind
until	basketball	fishpond	cold
public	handstand	insects	sprint
lunch	ball	paths	jump